baby bullfrogs

spoonbills

starlings

For John and Milo

The children featured in this book are from the Luo tribe of south-west Kenya.

*The wild creatures are the Citrus Swallowtail (butterfly), Striped Grass Mouse,
Yellow-headed Dwarf Gecko, Beautiful Sunbird, Armoured Ground Cricket,
(young) African Bullfrog, African Spoonbill and Superb Starling.*

*The author would like to thank everyone who helped her research this book,
in particular Joseph Ngetich from the Agricultural Office of the Kenya High Commission.*

Text and illustrations copyright © 2002 Eileen Browne
Dual Language copyright © 2003 Mantra Lingua
This edition published 2003
Published by arrangement with Walker Books Limited
London SE11 5HJ

British Library Cataloguing in Publication Data:
a catalogue record for this book is available from the British Library.

Published by
Mantra Lingua
5 Alexandra Grove, London N12 8NU
www.mantralingua.com

hen

butterflies

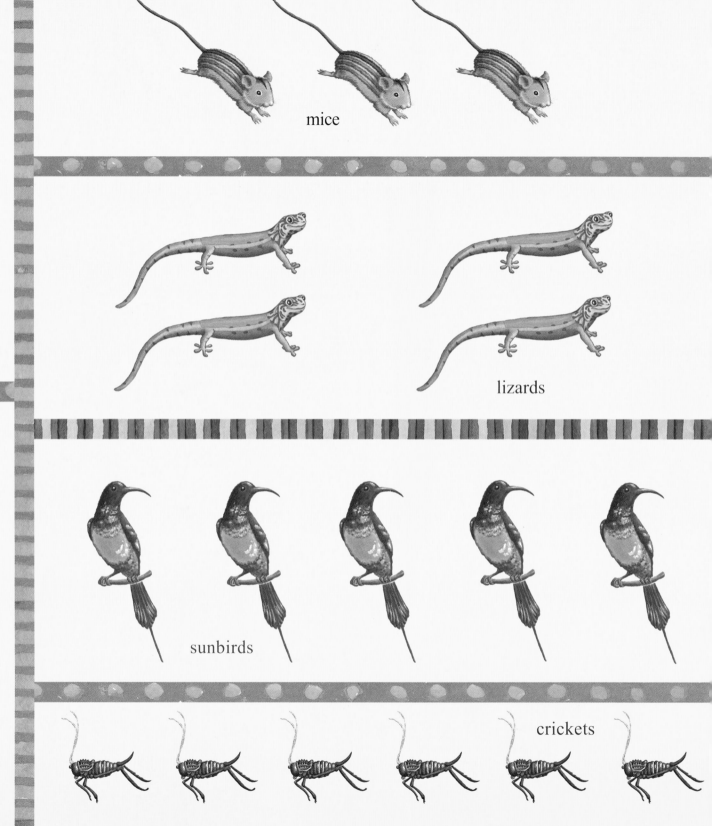

mice

lizards

sunbirds

crickets

韓達的母雞

Handa's Hen

Eileen Browne

Chinese translation by Sylvia Denham

mantra

韓達的祖母有一隻黑色的母雞，
她的名字叫夢迪－每天早上
韓達都會餵夢迪吃早餐。

Handa's grandma had one black hen.
Her name was Mondi - and every morning
Handa gave Mondi her breakfast.

有一日，夢迪沒有來吃東西。「祖母！」韓達叫道，「你見到夢迪嗎？」
「不，」祖母說，「但我卻見到你的朋友。」
「阿基奧！」韓達說，「請幫我一起找夢迪。」

One day, Mondi didn't come for her food. "Grandma!" called Handa. "Can you see Mondi?"
"No," said Grandma. "But I can see your friend."
"Akeyo!" said Handa. "Help me find Mondi."

韓達和阿基奧在雞屋的周圍找。
「看啊！ 兩隻拍翅震翼的蝴蝶，」阿基奧說。
「但是夢迪在那裏呢？」韓達說。

Handa and Akeyo hunted round the hen house.
"Look! Two fluttery butterflies," said Akeyo.
"But where's Mondi?" said Handa.

她們盯著穀倉的下面。
「噓！三隻有斑紋的小鼠，」阿基奧說。
「但是夢迪在那裏呢？」韓達說。

They peered under a grain store.
"Shh! Three stripy mice," said Akeyo.
"But where's Mondi?" said Handa.

她們窺探泥缸的後面。
「我可以見到四隻蜥蜴，」阿基奧說。
「但是夢迪在那裏呢？」韓達說。

They peeped behind some clay pots.
"I can see four little lizards," said Akeyo.
"But where's Mondi?" said Handa.

她們在一些正在開花的樹叢周圍找。
「五隻美麗的太陽鳥，」阿基奧說。
「但是夢迪在那裏呢？」韓達說。

They searched round some flowering trees.
"Five beautiful sunbirds," said Akeyo.
"But where's Mondi?" said Handa.

她們在長草叢中尋找。
「六隻蹦蹦跳的蟋蟀！」阿基奧說，「我們捉它們啊。」
「我想找夢迪呀。」韓達說。

They looked in the long, waving grass.
"Six jumpy crickets!" said Akeyo. "Let's catch them."
"I want to find Mondi," said Handa.

她們一直走到水坑。
「小牛蛙啊，」阿基奧說，「一共七隻！」

They went all the way down to the water hole.
"Baby bullfrogs," said Akeyo. "There are seven!"

「但是，在那裏...看呀！爪印啊！」韓達說。
她們跟隨著爪印追尋 ...

"But where's … oh look! Footprints!" said Handa.
They followed the footprints and found …

「只是有䴉鷺闊嘴鴨，」韓達說，「七隻... 不，是八隻，
但是夢迪在那裏？在那裏呢？」韓達說。

"Only spoonbills," said Handa. "Seven … no, eight.
But where, oh where is Mondi?"

「我希望她沒有被篦鷺闊嘴鴨吞了 –
或者被獅子吃了，」阿基奧說。

"I hope she hasn't been swallowed by a spoonbill -
or eaten by a lion," said Akeyo.

她們黯然地返回祖母處。
「那邊有－九隻閃亮的燕八哥呀！」阿基奧說。

Feeling sad, they went back towards Grandma's.
"Nine shiny starlings - over there!" said Akeyo.

「聽啊，」韓達說， 吱吱 吱吱 「那是什麼？」
吱吱 吱吱　　吱吱 吱吱　　　　吱吱 吱吱　　吱吱 吱吱
「是從樹叢下傳來的，我們去偷看好嗎？」

"Listen," said Handa. cheep cheep "What's that?"
cheep　　cheep　　cheep　　cheep
cheep　　cheep　　cheep　　cheep
"It's coming from under that bush. Shall we peep?"

韓達、阿基奧、夢迪和十隻小雞

Handa, Akeyo, Mondi and ten chicks

快步急跳著跑回祖母處 ...

hurried and scurried and skipped back to Grandma's ...

在那裏，他們全部都有一頓延遲了的早餐。

where they all had a very late breakfast.

hen

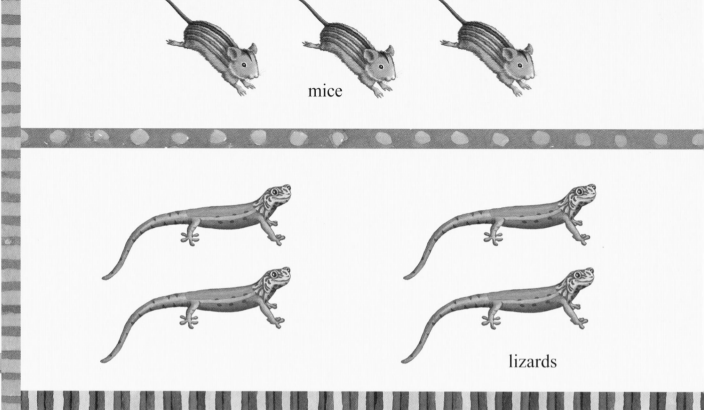

mice

lizards

butterflies

sunbirds

crickets

baby bullfrogs

spoonbills

starlings

chicks